THE FUNNIEST LEEDS QUOTES... EVER!

Also available

The Funniest Liverpool Quotes... Ever!

The Funniest Chelsea Quotes... Ever!

The Funniest West Ham Quotes... Ever!

The Funniest Spurs Quotes... Ever!

The Funniest Arsenal Quotes... Ever!

The Funniest Man City Quotes... Ever!

The Funniest Newcastle Quotes... Ever!

The Funniest United Quotes... Ever!

The Funniest Celtic Quotes... Ever!

The Funniest QPR Quotes... Ever!

The Funniest Everton Quotes... Ever!

The Funniest Rangers Quotes... Ever!

Mad All Over: The Funniest Crystal Palace Quotes... Ever!

Fergie Time: The Funniest Sir Alex Ferguson Quotes... Ever!

I Am The Normal One: The Funniest Jurgen Klopp Quotes... Ever!

I Didn't See It: The Funniest Arsene Wenger Quotes... Ever!

Zlatan Style: The Funniest Zlatan Ibrahimovic Quotes!

'Arry: The Funniest Harry Redknapp Quotes!

War of Words: The Funniest Neil Warnock Quotes!

Chuffed as a Badger: The Funniest Ian Holloway Quotes!

THE FUNNIEST LEEDS QUOTES... EVER!

by Gordon Law

Printed in Europe and the USA.
ISBN: 9781696966092
Imprint: Independently published

Photos courtesy of: Tomasz Bidermann/Shutterstock.com;
Maxisport/Shutterstock.com

Contents

Introduction

"I became a right idiot, someone who wasn't me. I had become a real rent-a-quote, never out of the papers."

That was David O'Leary's verdict on his final season at Leeds United with the manager's comical sound bites adding even more drama to the Elland Road soap opera.

The Irishman was a master at mixing up his metaphors, he loved referring to himself in the third person, while his constant referencing to "my babies" was the height of cringeworthy.

Howard Wilkinson was even more entertaining with his dour Yorkshire wit and array of hilarious analogies. Don Revie, Peter Reid and Neil Warnock were also noted for their bizarre pronouncements.

But the biggest motormouths could be found in the Leeds boardroom with the sharp tongue of chairman Ken Bates brilliantly taunting those who crossed him.

Controversial chief Massimo Cellino was also prone to some knockout verbals and bizarre statements like when he compared managers to watermelons, chosen for their good looks.

There have been gaffes from Paul Robinson and bloopers from Jonathan Woodgate to go with Gordon Strachan's pearls of wisdom.

Many of their foot-in-mouth moments and more can be found in this unique collection of funny Leeds quotes and I hope you laugh as much reading this book as I did in compiling it.

Gordon Law

THE FUNNIEST LEEDS QUOTES... EVER!

CALL THE MANAGER

THE FUNNIEST VILLA QUOTES... EVER!

"The referee must have felt like the President of the United States at the time of the Cuban missile crisis."

Howard Wilkinson after Leeds' game against Man United was cancelled due to a waterlogged pitch

"I gave him the heart attack because we were playing them off the park."

David O'Leary jokes about his friend Gerard Houllier who was taken ill at half-time

"At least all the aggravation will keep me slim."

George Graham on getting abuse from Tottenham fans

"I don't know why they don't have the bookings before the start so that we can get on with the game. You know they are coming."

David O'Leary on referee Mike Reed at Spurs

"I regretted not putting myself on the bench after 10 minutes of the game."

Neil Warnock on his first match as Leeds manager

"The third goal was in the net in the time it takes a snowflake to melt on a hot stove."

Howard Wilkinson on Tony Yeboah's hat-trick against Ipswich

"I said to the players at half-time, make it more entertaining. Let Liverpool get three goals and we will all go home happy."

Howard Wilkinson's sarcastic reply to critics of his negative tactics in a 3-0 cup defeat to Liverpool

"I believe when referees are enjoying their recreation on the sunbeds or swimming up and down the pool and talking together in their free time, there is an agenda with Alan Smith. They all have their little chats and jump on him very quickly."

David O'Leary after referee Andy D'Urso sent Smith off at Cardiff

"He went down like a ton of bricks like."

Neil Warnock on Chris Kirkland being attacked by a fan

"I've not enjoyed seeing a moron like that."

Warnock then strikes a different tone

"It was like being in the dentist's chair for six hours."

Howard Wilkinson after a clash with Leicester

"They're getting results doing it, but I'd rather watch paint dry."

Steve Evans on Forest's style of football

THE FUNNIEST LEEDS QUOTES... EVER!

"I'm healthy, I've got a house, I eat well – how can I be unhappy? There's thousands with none of these things."

Howard Wilkinson was asked by a reporter if he was unhappy after a bad result

"We've had three stone bonkers this season."

Terry Venables goes bonkers over three penalties Leeds should have been awarded

"I feel like Corky the Cat, who has been run over by a steamroller, got up and had someone punch him in the stomach."

Howard Wilkinson after Leeds were defeated by Arsenal in the FA Cup

"You only have to fart in the box to concede a penalty these days."

Kevin Blackwell on a spot-kick awarded to QPR

"I'll probably open a bottle of champagne tonight... I might even treat myself to a bag of crisps."

Neil Warnock after Leeds knock out Spurs in the FA Cup

"We let the convict out of jail and we know what they are like when they get free."

Howard Wilkinson after Leeds lose 3-0 against VfB Stuttgart

THE FUNNIEST LEEDS QUOTES... EVER!

"Going back to my Sunday League days I'd have been disappointed then to concede two or three of those goals."

Neil Warnock criticises his team's defending in a 7-3 defeat against Forest

"I'm feeling battered and bruised and more in need of recuperation than my players."

Howard Wilkinson after Leeds' 4-2 FA Cup win at Derby

"We had the babies looking after the young babies."

David O'Leary on bringing reserves in for an FA Cup clash

"Don't ask me whether it was a good game. It'd be like asking a surgeon if it was a good operation."

Howard Wilkinson

"It's not Brucey's fault his dad was the linesman!"

Peter Reid after Steve Bruce's Birmingham won 2-0 thanks to a re-taken penalty

"He's used to crowds. He's the youngest of 13 kids."

Howard Wilkinson on 19-year-old Gary Kelly's sparkling display at Man United

THE FUNNIEST LEEDS QUOTES... EVER!

FIELD OF DREAMS

"[Being a footballer] is the best job in the world. The second best is being a footballer's wife."

Gary McAllister

"There are some players in Scotland who are sick of the sight of me and I'm sick of the sight of them."

David Robertson on quitting Rangers for Leeds

"Once people left Manchester United, everyone used to think you went away, curled up and died... I didn't fancy that, dying a death at 32."

Gordon Strachan on departing for Leeds

"I room with Robbie Keane on away trips. If we're staying in a hotel on a Friday before a game we'll watch Trigger Happy TV, then So Graham Norton. After that we cuddle up and fall asleep. There's always the temptation of pay-per-view channels in the hotels but that would be embarrassing on your room bill."

Rio Ferdinand

"Leaving a club is like leaving a woman. When there's nothing left to say, you go."

Eric Cantona after joining Man United

"I was never any good at friendlies."

Norman Hunter

"We were frightened of nobody. Everybody was frightened of us – it was lovely!"

Jack Charlton

"I was thinking for the first 20 minutes, 'Bloody hell, what have I done?' I didn't see the ball, it was in the air for so long."

Gary McSheffrey reflects on League One football after joining Leeds on loan from Birmingham

"I don't think my girlfriend would be too happy to hear I've been chasing Totti around Rome."

Jonathan Woodgate before coming up against Roma's Francesco Totti

"What shirt am I wearing bruv? You serious?"
Jermaine Beckford responds to a reporter asking about his Leeds future

"I was in the Leeds end, chanting and going mad, and the fans were saying, 'Hold on, what's he doing here?'."
Noel Whelan

"All the Scotland posters in my room had been ripped down after the games against Peru and Iran. After that goal [Archie Gemmill's against Holland] they went back up."
Gary McAllister recalls the 1978 World Cup

"I told [the driving examiner] that I had put two of my cup final tickets in the glove box. He never said a word. I followed the route, and he informed me in a matter-of-fact way that I had passed the test. He then opened the glove box, took the tickets, and left."

Gary Sprake on how he passed his driving test, a few days before playing in the 1965 FA Cup Final

"I supported Motherwell as a kid, but whenever I'm linked with Rangers I'm a lifelong Rangers fan and when I was linked with Celtic I was a lifelong Celtic fan. I've supported lots of clubs if you believe the papers."

Gary McAllister

"In my early days at Leeds, when there were international games on, there'd be just me and Mick Bates left behind for training."

Trevor Cherry used to get a bit lonely

"I've played in a Champions League semi-final and a UEFA Cup semi-final, but this is a different game."

Eirik Bakke on the play-off final. Is it really?

"Leeds United? Most people imagine us an evil-looking bunch of characters with black capes and handlebar moustaches."

Johnny Giles

"I didn't think I deserved the vote, it is supposed to be for the worst trainer of the week. I wasn't even there for most of it as I was with the Republic of Ireland. I only trained last Friday and I wasn't bad on that day."

Ian Harte is still sore after winning the Robin Reliant award for the worst trainer and must drive one to the next home game

"I would not be bothered if we lost every game as long as we won the league."

Mark Viduka

"A tin pot side."

Paddy Kenny tweets about his last club QPR

"One club I would never consider joining is Manchester United."

Alan Smith in 2002 – two years before signing for United

"People hate Manchester United because they are so successful. People will hate us in a few years because we shall be winning everything."

Jonathan Woodgate is feeling confident

"If you ask any Leeds fan, they like it when they hear rival clubs chanting disrespectful things about them."

Richard Naylor

"I much prefer Flower of Scotland to Scotland the Brave as our pre-match anthem... I'm told Flower can be a bit politically insensitive – sending the English homeward to think again. But that doesn't stop Princess Anne belting it out at every rugby international."

Gary McAllister

Q: "Which team's results do you look for first?"

Jonathan Woodgate: "Leeds United, Leeds reserves, Leeds youth team, Leeds Permanent Building Society pub team, Leeds & Holbeck pub team, Leeds ice hockey team, East Leeds chess U19s, South Leeds over-19 poker team, anyone with Leeds in their name. And Middlesbrough."

"The only thing I miss about football is that feeling you get in the 10 seconds after you've scored, when you completely lose your head. I wouldn't say it's better than sex, but it's a close call."

Lee Chapman

"Music from the Victor Sylvester Dance Orchestra echoed across the pitch from the tannoy and we were ordered by the major to take our partners... The dancing was supposed to improve our rhythm and make us play like Brazilians. It didn't – we just fell about and he scrapped the idea in favour of hypnotism."

John Charles on 'Major' Frank Buckley's training programme

"It's weird, isn't it? I remember when a hundred quid seemed like a lot of money."

Jonathan Woodgate after Leeds splashed out £18m for Rio Ferdinand

"Fergie was doing an interview where he made it clear he felt we hadn't won it so much as United had lost it. I was watching in Lee Chapman's living room, waiting to be interviewed. I shouted, 'There he goes again, gracious as ever'. Denis Law came on in my earpiece and said, 'You do know he can hear you?' It's only now, 20 years later, that Fergie's speaking to me."

Gary McAllister on the 1992 title success

"I had a good memory of people who'd done nasty things to me. I'd get them back if I had the chance but I would do it within the laws of the game when the ball was there. I was a good tackler – you can tackle as hard as you like."

Jack Charlton

"I was in Pele's 100 players of the century. Not him [Steven Gerrard]. I respect him as a footballer, but there is nobody more egotistical than him. I spoke to the major figures at Liverpool and nobody can stand him."

El-Hadji Diouf blasts his old teammate

"English fans are brilliant. In England, when you ask someone which club he supports, it means something. The guy supports a club for his whole life, whatever the ups and downs."
Eric Cantona when asked about England fans rioting in Sweden

"Leeds is a great club and it's been my home for years, even though I live in Middlesbrough."
Jonathan Woodgate

"On the pitch, when I see green or smell green, I get a little bit crazy. The grass, you know? I get this green mist."
Jimmy Floyd Hasselbaink

"Sometimes driving home from a game, you do wonder if you're getting a bit old. But I always remember what Kenny Dalglish once told me: 'Never forget that football made you feel knackered when you were 17'."

Gordon Strachan

"I think of myself as one of the old guard. When I started playing you could kick owt that moved."

David Batty remembers the good ol' days

"Footballers are the worst gossips – they're worse than women."

Lee Chapman

"Do you think you'll be a player when your voice breaks?"

Billy Bremner to Alan Ball during Scotland's 1967 win over England

"I always dress from the left – left shin pad, left sock, left boot. It's stupid but I've always done it."

Paul Robinson

"I just hope everything will be OK because it is in the back of your mind that anything you do, you could pick up something."

Stephen McPhail on his trip to Nigeria with Ireland's U20s

"Look on the bright side, if your not getting played take the L out and get payed."

Ryan Hall – he ended up leaving the club by mutual consent

"This wasn't Wimbledon, where people tread on you like f*ckin' beetles. All of a sudden, when you walk through the jungle, you're this big f*ckin' white leopard! Someone that's respected."

Vinny Jones after joining Leeds

"My bum has been through every temperature known to man."

Gordon Strachan on the various wacky treatments he's been given over the years

"Our attitude was – an eye for an eyelash."

Johnny Giles

"The first day I went down for lunch, there was so much smoked salmon, steaks, king prawns, seven-inch-long langoustines, I asked David O'Leary and Eddie Gray who was getting married."

Greg Abbott on the free-spending days while working as youth coach

"This referee's so poor, I'd have been booked just getting off the coach."

Norman Hunter as a pundit on Mike Reed

"A snarling angry Alsatian was literally inches away from my thigh before the police handler grabbed his head and pulled him away. As I ran on I shouted over my shoulder, 'I only crossed the ball – it's Lee Chapman you want, he's the one that put your team down'."

Chris Kamara on the post-match pitch invasion after Leeds won promotion at Bournemouth, which relegated the Cherries

"I feel sh*t to be fair. I don't care, this was a robbery from the referee so it feels bad. Do you think I should be happy? No chance."

Pontus Jansson turns the air blue on live TV after Leeds' draw with Brentford

"Who writes this rubbish? What a load of sh*t this headline is. Never once mentioned I wasn't happy. Absolute clown whoever you are."

Stuart Dallas is angry about a headline that says he is "unhappy" under Marcelo Bielsa

"Yeah, I was a bit anxious when I got to the stadium. But in all fairness if I hadn't been anxious I'd have been worried."

Paul Robinson

"I went in for contract talks with Bill and came out with three season tickets and owing the club money."

Gordon Strachan on chairman Bill Fotherby

"In a really tight match one day against Chelsea at Elland Road, down near one of the corner flags, and with our backs to the referee, I caught [Eddie McCreadie] with a late tackle. 'What the hell was that for?' I told him it was for doing my ligaments at Stamford Bridge in 1964. McCreadie looked bewildered. It was 1972."

Johnny Giles

"They said, 'We've got to get four doctors. We need two to pull your arm that way and two more to pull it the other way'. And that's when I threw up."

Mick Jones on dislocating his arm during the 1972 FA Cup Final

"I didn't like the Leeds dressing room before games [in the Don Revie era]. Some guys would turn psycho, others would be physically sick and the goalie Gary Sprake got himself in a terrible state – his eyes actually started blinking on the Tuesday. Then there was Don with all his superstitions: lucky mohair suit with the a*se falling out, twice round his lucky lamp post and a final comb of the hair in the mirror."

Peter Lorimer

"I don't sit here and talk sh*t. I believe we will get in the play-offs and the other teams will shake a bit."

Pontus Jansson makes a strong statement about Leeds' promotion chances

"This is cup football now, it's all one-off games
– and we have two of them against Valencia."
Rio Ferdinand states the obvious

"I was on £500 a week and asked for two-and-
a-half grand, plus a BMW. With side skirts.
He never even twitched. I remember thinking
'F*ck. I could have doubled it'."
**Vinny Jones on negotiating his contract
with Peter Ridsdale**

"We should be in the top four with our squad.
We are 16th, just three points above the drop.
It's a disgrace."
Olivier Dacourt is not holding back

41

THE FUNNIEST LEEDS QUOTES... EVER!

LIFESTYLE CHOICE

"Players are no worse now than they were 30 years ago. It's getting to a stage where players will have to carry a contract in their pockets for girls to sign, saying that they consent to sex and won't go running to the papers."
Peter Lorimer, who once revealed he and seven players from the Scotland squad had sex with a woman during the World Cup

Waitress: "Would you like sugar?"
Neil Warnock: "You don't have sugar with a body like mine."
A common response from the Leeds manager in restaurants

"We were encouraged to open ourselves to the Japanese cuisine on offer. But having been away from home for so long I could have died for a McDonald's."

Danny Mills on the England squad's 2002 World Cup diet

"My wife was delighted when I went back to football because she could see I was bored. Suzannah and I have a great relationship that is built on laughter. I get out of bed every morning naked, she starts laughing, and we go from there."

Ken Bates

"Dogs are very honest. They'll never let you down. They'll play football with you in the garden... and at the end they'll crap all over your lawn."

Mark Viduka

"This place is for the haves and the 'have yachts'."

John Lukic ahead of Leeds' UEFA Cup tie with AS Monaco

"I am quite a gruesome person. I did have a scrapbook on the Yorkshire Ripper... That was one of my most treasured possessions."

David Batty

Lifestyle Choice

"Keep your hair short, your clothes smart and don't get caught up with loose girls."
Don Revie's advice to his squad

"Everything in my life happens very fast."
Kleberson told Leeds he wouldn't join them until his 15-year-old girlfriend – who he only met a year earlier – agreed to marry him and move to Yorkshire

Q: "What sporting event would you pay most to watch?"
A: "Someone absolutely mashing Prince Naseem Hamed."
David Hopkin

"The neighbours on one side have got a villa in Portugal, the other side have got a house in America. We're looking for one in Filey [Yorkshire]."
David Batty

"You go into a shop and it's just Armani this and that, and you buy it. Clothes you don't even need. I spent a grand once. Bit of a waste."
Gary Kelly

"Vinny Jones was no card player. We used to love having him around – by God did me and Imre Varadi take him for a few quid!"
Mel Sterland

"They tried to introduce me to Tetley's bitter when I first arrived. I never drank alcohol but it was too bitter for me so I couldn't handle it. They thought if you don't drink alcohol that you are not a real man."

Lucas Radebe

"My role, when I wasn't working the lathe, was that of general dogsbody and butt of jokes. Once I was told to go and fetch a bucket of steam. Another time it was a left-handed screwdriver. Being young and naive I actually went looking for them."

Norman Hunter on his first job working in an engineering works

"It's quite irritating to me that, having apparently been able to hit a football 300 yards, I can't do the same to a golf ball."

Peter Lorimer

"He may have had a bit of a weight problem. He liked his food and beer now and again, but he was one of the great guys."

Lee Chapman on Mel Sterland

"Gary Kelly is the maddest one at Leeds United. Without prompting he was climbing head first into wheelie bins."

Paul Robinson remembers a particular Christmas outing

Q: "Favourite drink?"

A: "Beer. No, I mean Coke."

Q: "Most prized possession?"

A: "My car."

Eirik Bakke in a programme interview, before being convicted of drink-driving

"When I lose, I've got to talk about it. I go home and relive it with the wife. She just nods and says, 'Yes' or 'No'."

Norman Hunter

"I earn more than all you w*nkers put together."

What Carlton Palmer apparently said to police after being arrested during a night out

"Mr Mandela is in fantastic shape for someone who is 82 years old – he moves faster than me!"

Lucas Radebe

"I do it at home, as well, strolling around like Tarzan in just a pair of Nikes. The neighbours know me pretty well."

Gary Kelly on ironing in the nude – and even in his hotel room for away matches

"Duran Duran? I like all their songs, especially Rio, although, obviously, I can't sing that too loudly around the training ground now."

Mark Viduka

"It was all that leek and potato soup I was brought up on in Wales."

Gary Speed reveals the secrets of his longevity

"I've never had a drink, never, not once. I'm teetotal. The girlfriend does, mind, she drinks for us both."

Alan Smith

"The lifestyle is much the same – bad clothing, bad food – so we don't expect too much."

Alf-Inge Haaland explains why Norwegians adapt so well to England

THE FUNNIEST LEEDS QUOTES... EVER!

BOARDROOM
BANTER

"George [Graham] knew where London was when he signed his new contract last December. We haven't moved the Elland Road ground over the last 12 months."
Peter Ridsdale after the manager said he wanted to go back to the capital

"If I had my time over again, I'd be a general or a bishop."
Ken Bates

"There's more chance of us signing Father Christmas than Robbie Fowler."
Peter Ridsdale – the striker joined less than a year later

"I pay millions and millions at clubs and [the courts] say I tried to screw them over for a small amount. It's stupid. I could pay that tomorrow. I am not a dishonest crook. If I made a mistake it was not on purpose... I'm so shocked and ashamed that I feel like I will jump from the window right now."

Massimo Cellino after he fails the Football League's 'fit and proper person' test when trying to buy Leeds. He had been found guilty of avoiding £325,000 in tax in Italy

"Cashley Cole has publicly stated that he hates England (and the English). I suppose Cheryl thinks the same about you, 'Cashley'."

Ken Bates hits out at Ashley Cole

"If it is a case of losing 10,000 season tickets versus the £9m we have just generated from Jonathan Woodgate, then there is no discussion."

Peter Ridsdale makes himself popular with the fans

"I genuinely thought when Abramovich bought the club that he would use his money to accelerate down the road I was already on. Instead he went mad. I said to them, 'Man United must be laughing their f*cking socks off. [Juan Sebastian] Veron and [Peter] Kenyon... they've sold you two lemons in three weeks.'"

Ken Bates on selling Chelsea to Roman Abramovich

"The players p*ssed me off because they didn't fight for the club. They made the fans feel ashamed. For what they did, I would kick their a*ses one by one. They are guilty. They were without pride and should be ashamed of themselves. They are chickens."

Massimo Cellino after a 5-1 loss at home to Bolton, shortly becoming club owner

"Free tickets? They cost the fans who can't afford holidays. When Tony Blair and his wife were guests of honour at Wembley, we got a request for five free tickets! I told them to f*ck off."

Ken Bates on Tony Blair

"Now we are treading water. In a year's time I hope to have one foot on the sand, which is where we want to be as quickly as possible. And following that, I would hope to be on the sand running with a blonde."
John McKenzie

"We had a couple of tantrums from the visiting manager... who made much out of his failure to take his little boy on the pitch, apparently confusing the football ground with a playground."
Ken Bates criticises Derby manager Nigel Clough who was unhappy his son was not allowed to walk on the Leeds pitch

"OK, they cost us £20 a month to hire, but they were in the club colours of blue and yellow."
Peter Ridsdale on the infamous goldfish in his office

"There are no more goldfish. I ate them with my tuna sandwich at lunch."
Gerald Krasner says Ridsdale's fish are gone

"There's nothing else in life except soccer and a good woman. I've got a good woman so I need the soccer."
Ken Bates on why he became Leeds chief

"Jonathan [Woodgate] is a world-class defender but could never be described as a mastermind. He had been told to look after his own passport and 'to keep it somewhere safe'. On one European trip the players were asked for their passports. Jonathan hadn't brought it with him. 'Where is it?' I asked him. 'You told me to put it somewhere safe so I did. It's in the safe at home'."

Peter Ridsdale

"Now, if you could just let us have your names and those of your newspapers, we'll know who to ban."

Ken Bates at the end of his first press conference as chairman in 2005

"Some fans said, 'We don't want a bloody Londoner running Leeds'. I said you've got a problem then, haven't you? Nobody in Leeds wants to run Leeds, do they? I see all these bloody millionaires with money coming out of their ears. Talk about long pockets and short hands."

Ken Bates

"Having 30 Premier League footballers in a city, buying dinner and gifts, is like having 30 small businesses."

Adam Pearson, the ex-Leeds commercial director, on the city needing to have a club in the top division

"He doesn't give a f*ck. He didn't show up to training. He didn't fly with the club to pre-season. I was so p*ssed off that when Fulham called me I asked them for £10m to make them not buy the player. They said yes! Bloody hell."

Massimo Cellino on Ross McCormack

"Everyone wants to speak to me now that I've got money."

Ken Bates on a visit to Liverpool after selling the club

"I don't need to kiss the ass of anyone, I am driving this bus."

Massimo Cellino

"It's like an oil tanker that's heading for the rocks... The trouble with oil tankers is they're two miles long and they don't turn around in two minutes."

John McKenzie on taking over as chairman

"The coverage was absolutely dreadful and amateurish. On the technical side, nobody had the wit to wipe the lenses clean of the rain, it was like watching through a fish pond. I think the people who run Strictly Come Dancing probably did it rather than anybody to do with football."

Ken Bates on the ITV presentation of Leeds' shock FA Cup defeat by Histon

"I told him, 'Widen your horizons, leave your provincial town and come to Leeds'. I said I could only offer a grand a week and all the Yorkshire pudding he could eat. Sadly, he chose money above fame. He will never know the thrill of playing at Yeovil, Darlington and Wycombe."

Ken Bates on trying to sign Steven Gerrard

"He's a very cool guy. I don't know why (I have chosen him). Coaches are like watermelon. You find out about them when you open them. His particular qualities? He's good looking."

Massimo Cellino on new manager Darko Milanic – he lasted just six games

"When I left Leeds I had two options – to jump off the top of a tall building or to cope. I decided to cope."

Peter Ridsdale on taking over at Cardiff City

"Leeds is the only city outside of Exeter that only had one senior football club, which I found amazing."

Ken Bates forgets about the likes of Newcastle, Leicester, Southampton...

"Rio Ferdinand is going nowhere. Where does he think he is going – into thin air?"

Peter Ridsdale – a big transfer to Man United went through days later

"If Man City do the treble this year, big bloody deal. So what. What have they achieved? F*ck all."

Ken Bates

"I think somebody went too far. To show the manager as a gorilla was offensive, I think."

John McKenzie after a Fiat advertisement took the mickey out of Peter Reid

"The gravy train hit the f*cking buffers but the passengers kept eating."

Ken Bates on how Leeds ran out of cash

"[Leeds United] remind me of a young Pamela Anderson – in great shape, with superb assets and a great future ahead."

David Haugh, the chief exec of GFH Capital, which bought Leeds from Ken Bates in 2012

"The thing the three of them have in common is that they are not British and all they appear to want to do is what's best for their wallets."

Peter Ridsdale on Jimmy Floyd Hasselbaink, Nicolas Anelka and Pierre van Hooijdonk

"Who does he play for? I've only ever heard of his brother, Ukelele."

Ken Bates on Claude Makelele

"We lived the dream."

Peter Ridsdale on writing cheques for David O'Leary

"Leeds United may have lived the dream, but I inherited the nightmare."

John McKenzie

"It's too simple to sack David Hockaday. The squad isn't finished. That's my fault, so if I fire anyone, I should fire myself, or else I'm a coward. I have to control my ego."

Massimo Cellino – before firing Hockaday

"Don't get excited about Jermaine Beckford's transfer request, he handed that in a fortnight ago! So it's no surprise to us."

Ken Bates seems to be ignoring the player's demand

"Peter Ridsdale has had the bottle to push on rather than consolidate."

Adam Pearson, the Leeds commercial director, doesn't quite get it

"It's better than lying in bed, drinking gin and tonic and waiting to die."

Ken Bates on Leeds' financial troubles

"Ninety-nine per cent of the letters and emails [from fans] are supporting us. That's as good as Saddam Hussein got – and he was fiddling the figures."

Ken Bates after buying Leeds back from the administrators in 2007

"I was raised as a manager, not as a bullsh*t president who puts his tie on, eats some roast beef and f*cks off home. I look after everything. In 2015/16, if we don't go into the Premier League then I've failed. You can tell me I've failed."

New owner Massimo Cellino

"I had more or less 50 coaches in my existence, they are all the same. I used to have a boat, I used to pay the captain of the boat. You know what my strategy was? If he doesn't do what I like to do with my boat, then I can drive my boat on my own."

Massimo Cellino

"There's a picture of a fish tank in the offices downstairs. It symbolises what happened here a decade ago. It acts as a reminder, like taking a picture of yourself in Speedos and sticking it on the fridge door so you don't eat that extra slice of cake."

Managing director David Haigh

"David Hockaday, the first day he heard [Ross] McCormack wanted to go he said, 'I don't want him in pre-season, sell him'. I told Hockaday, 'Did I ask your f*cking advice? No. So shut the f*ck up'."

Massimo Cellino

"Let us leave the EEC, abolish human rights laws, take TV sets, pool tables and phones out of prisons, bring back corporal and capital punishment, slash benefits and put single mothers into hostels instead of giving them council flats. Finally, if we chucked out all the illegal immigrants and asylum seekers there would be enough jobs for everyone."

Ken Bates rants in his programme notes

"Don't forget where he came from; league five. Talking with managers of Premier League clubs, Championship clubs, is a new thing. He's like a baby, who is in a toy shop."

Massimo Cellino patronises Dave Hockaday

"[Alex] Ferguson's not very likeable, and I dislike [Arsene] Wenger immensely, but you have to admire what they've done."

Ken Bates sits on the fence as ever

"I have been proud to work at Leeds United, with nice people. If you can survive working with me, you can survive anything!"

Massimo Cellino after leaving the club

THE FUNNIEST LEEDS QUOTES... EVER!

MANAGING JUST FINE

"It is not illegal, we have been doing it publicly and we talk about it in the press. For some people, it's the wrong thing to do and for other people, it's not the wrong thing to do."

Marcelo Bielsa makes a stunning admission that Leeds spied on a Derby training sesssion

"The Championship is a hard league and you're playing against different opposition every week."

Neil Warnock

"Achilles tendon injuries are the worst you can probably have – they are a pain in the butt."

David O'Leary

"I read the papers and they said we played badly last week. I thought we were fantastic, so it shows how much I know."

David O'Leary

"My old mate Colin Harvey, who coaches the kids at Everton, is not one to go overboard. He described Kenny Dalglish as 'all right' but Rooney as 'a good player'."

Caretaker boss Peter Reid

"We're not a selling club any more. If we still had the goldfish we would keep them now. Unfortunately, we had to eat them."

Kevin Blackwell

"There have always been hooligans. In Germany they were the Gestapo and in Russia they were in the KGB."

Howard Wilkinson after trouble by Leeds fans at Bournemouth in 1990

"Then there is Stephen Warnock. There is an obvious temptation to sign him – if the fans start chanting 'Warnock out' I'll take him off."

Neil Warnock on new signings

"The club is like an old Savile Row suit, frayed at the edges. Like a Rolls Royce in a breakers yard."

Howard Wilkinson on arriving at Leeds

"If I was a child, I would say I won't do it again, but I wouldn't feel right responding like this and would lose credibility. I won't say that I won't do it again. It's a childish position to answer like that."

Marcelo Bielsa is unapologetic about 'Spygate'

"I'm so old I can even remember the days when tackling was allowed in this sport."

Peter Reid

"I've never known a club like it. If it can go wrong, it will go wrong."

Kevin Blackwell

"You don't like Batesy and you don't particularly like me, but at the end of the day... you've got us."

Dennis Wise to the Leeds fans

"You wonder how someone could have come up with a plan straight out of Blackadder. You can see Baldrick: 'I've got a cunning plan that'll take us further into debt'."

Kevin Blackwell on the Peter Ridsdale era

"The big-city team with the small-town mentality."

Howard Wilkinson on former club Sheffield Wednesday

"I haven't thought about shaking hands yet. But I don't think I should get into that because the last time I heard from Rafa he was threatening to sue me if I mentioned [the row] again. It was an email and I think it was his solicitor who was threatening legal action but I think it had Rafa's name on it. I've got it in a scrapbook at home."

Neil Warnock is unsure if he'll get a frosty reception from Chelsea interim boss Rafa Benitez after having a previous bust-up

"I think the only people we have not been involved with in going through from the qualifying rounds to the semi-final are NATO."

David O'Leary on the Champions League

"If people feel that they don't want to be part of what we are doing here, then I won't kiss their rears to keep them."

David O'Leary

"Being top won't change much. It'll probably rain tomorrow and the traffic lights will still be red."

Howard Wilkinson on being at the summit for the first time since 1991

"None of the sharks will be getting at my babies for the time being, and I've told my babies that."

David O'Leary

"There's no doubt we'll be seen as a big fish in the First Division – everybody will be trying to knock us off our perch."

Kevin Blackwell. Fish and perch?

"My father and mother had a mixed marriage: Liverpool and Everton. There were always rucks. I can't believe they're still together."

Peter Reid

"Ips... Wsspw... Isspitch... Isswitch... OK, I give up!"

Marcelo Bielsa struggles to pronounce opponents Ipswich

"You can say it's a club that's sinking but it's Leeds United – it's a liner, not a canoe."

Peter Reid looks for the lifeboats

"We'll take support whether it's Kent or the Arctic Circle."

Kevin Blackwell

"He said Andrew Umbers is coming to the game and he's bringing his wife. His wife has never seen us win. You need to get something lucky. You need to wear something purple – socks or a belt. Or you need to shake Eddie Gray's hand, he was born on the 17th."

Neil Redfearn on Massimo Cellino

"To put it in working-class terms, they stopped rolling their sleeves up and getting their knees dirty."

Howard Wilkinson on Leeds' fall from grace

"As soon as you think you have turned a corner you end up hitting something coming around that corner."

Terry Venables is full of positivity

"I hope Leeds win today because of those players down there, because most of them, in the nicest possible way, are mine."

David O'Leary – can someone tell him he's no longer the manager

"A myth has grown up that football should in some way strive to be entertaining. Sport is not entertainment. It's an activity for the benefit of the participants. If you run away from that you risk having the wrong pipers calling the tune."

Howard Wilkinson

"I think the foundations of that empire have now been laid."

David O'Leary just over a year into his tenure

"One boozy night has brought this club down."

David O'Leary at the end

"Manchester United have been exceptional for 10 years – but I've not seen anything as good as that."

Terry Venables. Erm?

"I told the players I want them to be a bit like the Leeds of before who were... Well, 'orrible. I want a bit of nastiness, like they used to have here."

Dennis Wise

"Whose is it?"

When coach Les Cocker was told that Norman Hunter had broken a leg

"There are two ways of getting the ball. One is from your own teammates, and that's the only way."

Terry Venables

"Right you f*cking lot, as far as I'm concerned you can take all the medals you have won and throw them in that bin over there."

Brian Clough on his first day as Leeds boss

"He was getting rid of people on £12k a year and still paying Paddy Kenny, who couldn't stop a pig in a passage, £20k a week."

Neil Redfearn on Massimo Cellino

"Fifty euros was all I came out with. I'd have given them more if I'd had it. I feel a bit bad actually."

Brian McDermott gave some Leeds fans the last €50 in his pocket on a pre-season tour in Slovenia

"On my children's lives – and I don't think I'm a thick person – I didn't have a clue about the financial state of the club."

David O'Leary

"He could sell sand to the Arabs."

Howard Wilkinson on chairman Bill Fotherby

CALLING THE SHOTS

"He's played with swollen ankles, with pulls, with colds, with his legs black and blue. He's turned out with knocks, with strains, with cuts. So determined is Norman [Hunter] that never once has he said he is unfit."

Don Revie

"Once Tony Daley opens his legs, you're in trouble."

Howard Wilkinson

"I think he thought he was a Zidane. He wasn't. He was also a very cold fish."

David O'Leary on Harry Kewell

"I don't know how it could have happened. I can't imagine him jumping for a ball. One of his false eyelashes might come out... I wouldn't know if he was match fit, I've never seen him fit."

George Graham on a head injury suffered by former Leeds striker Tomas Brolin while playing for Palace

"He can destroy at once the big tough guys in the dressing room with one lash of his coruscating tongue. That's why he earned the nickname King Tongue."

Howard Wilkinson on Gordon Strachan

"When I say nice things to him, he understands me very well. When I suggest he works harder, he finds it more difficult."

Howard Wilkinson on Eric Cantona's understanding of the English language

Gary Lineker: "Do you think Rio Ferdinand is a natural defender?"

David O'Leary: "He could grow into one."

During BBC's 2002 World Cup coverage

"When he plays on snow, he doesn't leave any footprints."

Don Revie on Eddie Gray

"We frighten people by putting the ball into the net here."

Howard Wilkinson to Vinnie Jones when he joined Leeds

"I want Lee Bowyer to stay here. It would be a massive kick in the teeth if he ended up not signing this new contract."

David O'Leary's interesting choice of words for the player

"Quite frankly, I would rather have anyone in any position in my team who wanted to do well for Leeds United than someone who didn't."

Howard Wilkinson has a dig at Tomas Brolin

Brian Clough: "Hunter, you're a dirty b*stard and everyone hates you. I know everyone likes to be loved, and you'd like to be loved too, wouldn't you?"

Norman Hunter: "Actually, I couldn't give a f*ck."

"Mark Viduka had his own way. He knew if some-one was talking shit – he'd see through them."

David O'Leary

"Journalists arrived from all over Europe to meet him [Eric Cantona]. He gave interviews on art, philosophy and politics. A natural room-mate for David Batty, I thought immediately."

Howard Wilkinson

Peter Reid: "What did you think of the Man United game yesterday?"

Mark Viduka: "Dunno, I didn't watch. I don't really like football."

"The only thing you realise, it's a good job his career is in football and not in singing."

Steve Evans on Sol Bamba joining in with the fan chants

"Eric [Cantona] likes to do what he likes, when he likes, because he likes it – and then f*ck off. We'd all want a bit of that."

Howard Wilkinson after selling the Frenchman

THE FUNNIEST LEEDS QUOTES... EVER!

TALKING BALLS

"He's only selling me so he'll look good to the fans."

Paul Robinson criticises chairman John McKenzie. Shortly after he was back at Leeds when a move to Aston Villa collapsed

"He disliked personalities who had a rapport with the fans."

Eric Cantona on Howard Wilkinson

"I got on with Jimmy Adamson. He was a strange fellow, though. He had Dave Merrington as his No.2 and he was a total nutcase, too."

Tony Currie

"Ken Bates has been great. We don't have much day-to-day involvement with him – he is probably sitting on his yacht somewhere while we are back in sunny Leeds. Hopefully we may get an invite to the yacht if we win promotion – that would be superb."

Shaun Derry

"I have been here at Leeds for two years and he hasn't spoken much to me."

Mark Viduka on compatriot Harry Kewell

"Jack [Charlton] is not always right, but he is never wrong."

Johnny Giles on his old teammate

"The kids came through from the swimming pool and said that Leeds had signed Vinnie Jones. I started laughing and they said no, it was serious. I leapt into the pool, but thought, 'There's no point in drowning yourself, you're getting well paid'."

Gordon Strachan

"Dennis Wise said although I was talented, that I was 'French and a little bit lazy!'"

Seb Carole

"At the end of [Howard] Wilkinson's team talks we'd be thinking, 'Eh?'"

David Batty

"I had conversations with him that left me bamboozled. He was saying things that I didn't understand. I was left gobsmacked half the time. I would just shake my head and think, 'What?'. He was my boss and I couldn't argue with him, but I just used to sit there in disbelief."

Harry Kewell on David O'Leary

"I was not disappointed to see him get the sack."

Kewell continues on O'Leary

"After losing my front teeth there was nothing holding me back."

Joe Jordan

"The boss said to me, 'If you screw the nut and do what we tell you, then you could play for England'. I did and he was correct."

Jack Charlton on Don Revie

"Ken Bates has never been afraid to shirk any responsibilities."

Norman Hunter actually tries to praise Leeds' new owner

"I can never remember Don Revie telling us to go out and kick anybody. All he used to say to me was, 'Norman, let them know you're there – first tackle'!"

Norman Hunter

"I don't think I'd be as hard as Norman [Hunter] but certainly if it came to the real deadly stuff then I would be more dangerous."
Johnny Giles

"He isn't the tallest, but he jumps as though he's on a trampoline."
Steve Stone after Alan Wright joins on loan from Sheffield United

"Would anybody be happy if their boss walked into the middle of the office and started having a go at them?"
Danny Mills on David O'Leary

"His comments were strange and rather incoherent. One moment he would tell me that he wants me to know that I owe everything to him, that I am only a Frenchman lost in the English league. And at other times he would say that without me, the team is nothing."

Eric Cantona on Howard Wilkinson

"He was a rude b*stard, and arrogant – but that was part of his genius."

Johnny Giles on Brian Clough

"In six months he said just two words to me: 'You're fired'."

Tomas Brolin on George Graham

"He would sit in a comfy chair in his office, cardigan and slippers on, smoking a pipe. Once he dropped me and I went to ask him why. He said, 'Brian, I didn't drop you. I just picked someone else'."

Brian Flynn on Jimmy Armfield

"You're not here to kill people, you're here because we know you're a good player."

Gordon Strachan to Vinny Jones

"Lock that boy up in a cage and throw away the key until he's a Leeds player."

Jack Charlton on teenage trialist Eddie Gray

"If teams knew Ian Baird was playing, it wasn't shin pads they reached for, it was gum shields."
Ian Snodin

"My toes are like horrible wee bits and bobs. It scares people on the beach as I walk along in my thong."
Gordon Strachan had his toe nails pulled out as it was causing him trouble

"I know it sounds nuts, but I thought I was signing for Howard Kendall. He was the only Howard I'd really heard of."
Vinnie Jones on Howard Wilkinson

"Don Revie used to tell us to go in hard with the first tackle, because the referee would never book you for the first one. We used to call it the freebie. I'd go in hard, pick 'em up, say sorry to the ref and sometimes you hardly saw that player again."

Norman Hunter

"He's very fit, very fit for his age... Unbelievable. He is Forrest Gump!"

Olivier Dacourt on Eddie Gray

"I came back last season with blond hair and I think that did his head in."

Lee Sharpe on George Graham

"It's a tremendous honour. I'm going to have a banana to celebrate."

Gordon Strachan on being named Footballer of the Year in 1991

"I don't mind if someone says to me, 'You were a dirty little b*stard'. I don't mind that. But please say, 'You could play a bit'."

Johnny Giles

Tony Dorigo: "Your tracksuit is disgusting."

David Batty: "It's not mine, it's yours."

Batty returned to their hotel room on England duty, covered in blood and guts from fishing

"I know probably this team needs a better player than me but I just want to play and do my best every Saturday."

Gaetano Berardi's astonishing admission that the club should replace him

"[Howard Wilkinson] said, 'I'm disappointed in you. I've just been in there, and there's no blood'. That's what he said! I'm like, 'What do you mean?' And he said 'Why do you think I brought you to this club? To sort those f*cking w*nkers out'."

Vinny Jones on smacking Bobby Davison and Ian Baird in the players' lounge after they criticised him

CAN YOU MANAGE?

"I saw Ron Greenwood break out in sores, Bobby Robson go grey and poor Graham Taylor double up in anguish and stick his head so far between his legs that it nearly disappeared up his backside. If I was single, with no kids, it'd be no problem. But I've a wife and three children and I've seen how this job can affect your family. It won't happen to mine."

Howard Wilkinson after Graham Taylor's departure from the England job

"I like Jimmy but I wouldn't go on the dole for him."

David O'Leary on reports he would leave if Jimmy Floyd Hasselbaink was sold

"It's not for me to tell [Fabio] Capello his job. Otherwise, I'd probably have got him to the World Cup final."

Neil Warnock rates his ability

"I'm not going to put a list of players together and give it to the president. Because if I just wanted to write a list of players, I'd have Cristiano Ronaldo on it, wouldn't I?"

Steve Evans

"Life has to be lived forwards, but can only be viewed backwards."

Howard Wilkinson

"I'm not a politician, a social worker or clergyman. I'm a provider of distraction and fans want to go home happy to whatever bores the a*se off them during the week."
Howard Wilkinson

"Now I think I'm good, but I don't think I'm a genius. Paul Daniels would have a good job here, I tell you."
Kevin Blackwell

"I've been treated like a patsy."
Terry Venables considers his future after the sale of Jonathan Woodgate

"A manager is not self-employed. If he's not in the directors' hands, he's in the players' hands. And if he's not in the players' hands, he's in the fans' hands."

Howard Wilkinson had seen it coming...

"There's only two types of manager. Those who have been sacked and those who will be sacked in the future."

Wilkinson, just before getting fired

"David O'Leary may be a crap manager, but he is honest."

The manager refers to himself in the third person

"I'd like to create a more approachable personality for myself. If I'm ever reincarnated, I'd like
to return as a personality."

Howard Wilkinson

"Not only have they taken my arms and legs
off, now they've cut my balls off as well."

**Dennis Wise after the Football League
upheld the 15-point deduction**

"It's Christmas, babies being born and wedding
day rolled into one."

**Steve Evans on his excitement at being
named Leeds manager**

"It wasn't me that ran up a debt of £40m, £50m, £60m or £80m. I didn't force [Leeds] to sign one player. I nominated players and the club sorted out the wages."

David O'Leary

"It's like saying that to be a top jockey you need to have been a horse."

Howard Wilkinson refutes the idea that the next England manager should have played international football

"I was a young lad when I was growing up."

David O'Leary

THE FUNNIEST LEEDS QUOTES... EVER!

FAN FRENZY

"He's here, he's there, he wears no underwear, Lee Bowyer, Lee Bowyer."

Leeds fans after the midfielder revealed he likes to go 'commando'

"15 points, who gives a f*ck? We're super Leeds, and we're going up!"

The supporters in optimistic mood after the 15-point penalty

"Here for the shot-put, we're only here for the shot-put."

Leeds were losing 4-1 at Rotherham's Don Valley athletics stadium

Fan Frenzy

"Three more points to go, then we get to zero."

On getting to minus three points to the tune of '10 Men Went To Mow'

"Zero! Zero! Zero!"

Jubilation after Leeds' two-goal win against Hartlepool took them back to zero points

"Wembley, Wembley, we're the famous Leeds United and we're off to win some paint!"

The supporters look on the bright side of relegation to League One and entry to the Johnstone's Paint Trophy

"When you've just bought a club and go straight to the pub, that's Cellino."

The fans on new owner Massimo Cellino who popped into the Old Peacock on his first day as owner

"Oh my God I can't believe it, we've never been this good away from home!"

Whites fans to the tune of the Kaiser Chiefs' 'Oh My God'

"You should have watched on Setanta!"

To the Northampton fans whose team were being thrashed in an FA Cup replay

Fan Frenzy

"You are my Kandol, my Tresor Kandol, you signed from Barnet, on deadline day.
We did not notice, that you could score goals, until that day at Tranmere away."

A little ditty for the striker to the tune of 'You Are My Sunshine'

"Face like a donkey, you've got a face like a donkey."

Aimed towards Ruud van Nistelrooy

"We've got McAllister, you've got chlamydia."

Leeds fans at Peterborough where there were two mobile STI testing vans outside the ground

"Brian Deane, Brian Deane spies the Man U net. Brian Deane, Brian Deane, Fergie's in a sweat. In off the bar, f*ck Cantona, Brian Deane, Brian Deane. Brian Deane."

To the tune of Robin Hood

"Cellino... He comes from Italy – he don't pay VAT!"

An ode to the club's new owner, who failed to pay VAT on an imported Range Rover

"We are humans, we are humans, we are humans."

In response to the Wolves chant of: "We are Wolves, we are Wolves, we are Wolves"

"Ten men... We've only got 10 men..."

After a player from Leeds Ladies is subbed on in Lucas Radebe's testimonial

"All of the spies are hidden away, just try not to worry, you'll beat us some day. We beat you at home, we beat you away. Stop crying Frank Lampard."

To Derby manager Frank Lampard who had complained about the 'Spygate' controversy to the song 'Stop Crying Your Heart Out'

"Town full of sea men, you're just a town full of sea men."

To Plymouth Argyle supporters